Pepper

Illustrations by Beth McFall

Collins Colour Cubs

One morning Wil was dreaming of a large bowl of snails, and coming towards him was the biggest snail you ever saw! Wil's tongue stuck to the roof of his mouth in fear.

The snail came nearer and nearer with its mouth open until a cold sweat broke out on Wil's brow. It stretched its horns around Wil's neck and shouted, "Wil! Wil! Eating snails, is it?"
"Quack! I won't eat snails again, I promise! Quack!"

"Eating snails? What's the matter, little Wil?"
He knew that voice – the voice of Martha his mother. "Dreaming again, my boy?"
"Quack! Yes, Mam," and he gave her a big kiss.
She blushed, "Oh tut! Go on with you! Your breakfast is ready, and your friends are waiting for you."

In a jiffy Wil was out of bed and changing his clothes and half-flying half-running downstairs to the kitchen.

"Hey, little Cwac, eat your breakfast!"
Wil swallowed his wasp porridge, "Shlup aah!" and hurried out, slamming the door.
"Thanks, Mam! Morning Dad!"
"Oh! You wait! You naughty little Cwac!"

When Wil glanced back through the window and saw his father all covered with pepper he decided it was time to disappear. "Hullo, lads! Follow me to the woods!"

When they'd gone far enough, Dic said, "Stop, stop Wil, I'm . . . I'm puffed."
And Huw said, "Hey Wil, what was that strange noise from your house?"
"Oh, that was Dad sneezing because I knocked the pepper pot all over him."

"Gobble gobble Wil!" laughed Ifan.
"Pepper? Oh Wil!"
"You'll get a hiding!"
"And go to bed without supper!"
"Quack! Do you think so, lads?"
"Yes, of course," said Shoni, and winked at Ifan. "Waw! What's that terrible sound?"
"What sound?"
"Sounds like sneezing, gobble gobble, coming nearer and nearer!"

"Great snails! It's my Dad. Hide me, quack!"
"Hurry, let's jump on him," shouted Shoni, and in a twinkling they all leaped on Wil and sat on him, until he was out of sight.

But Shoni's tail tickled Wil's nose and Wil sneezed violently throwing the others off. When Wil saw the others laughing he realised that they'd tricked him and he began to laugh too.

But – oh dear! The laughter didn't last long because when Wil sneezed he'd thrown Shoni against a nest of bees, who came out angrily and made a bee-line for the boys.

They all howled as they fled down the path with the bees after them. "Help! Gobble gobble! Ouch!"

They went down into the yard and dived into Martha's washtub full of soapy water. When Martha came to see the commotion, she had to shut the door quickly, and all she and Wil's Dad could do was to look through the window.

At last the bees grew tired and flew back to the woods. And then Wil's Mam and Dad came out to the yard. But there was such a miserable look on the faces of the boys that Wil's Dad simply couldn't give Wil a row.

And they all had to stand under the pump and be washed clean. Then Martha gave them a dose of lamp oil, soot and black ink.

And when Wil went to bed that night, he swore that he'd look carefully next time before slamming the door . . .
"Goodnight . . . Quack!"